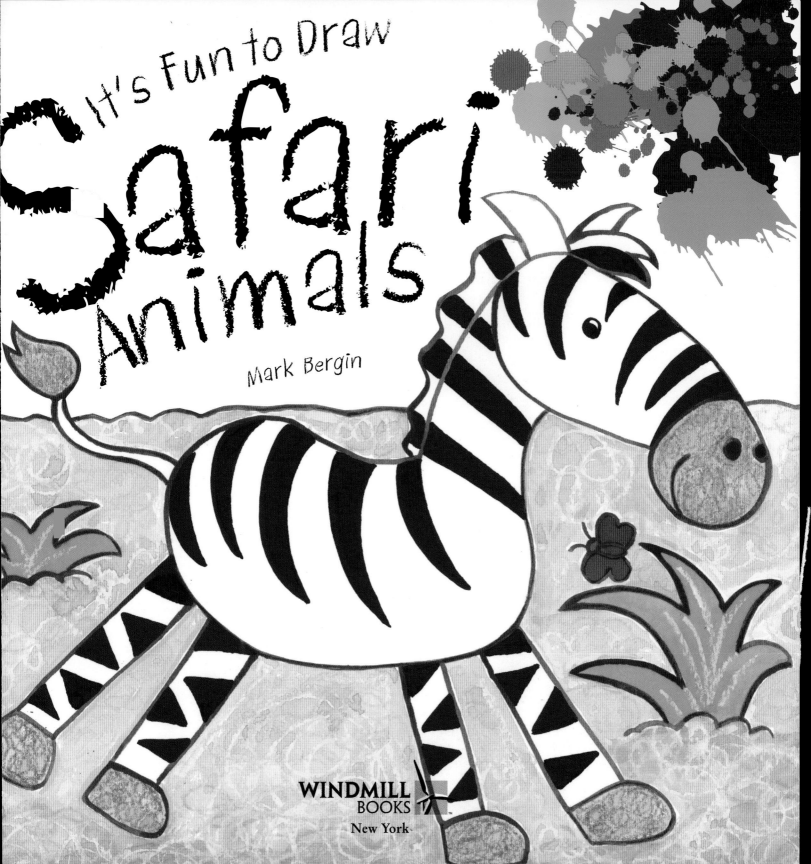

It's Fun to Draw

Safari
Animals

Mark Bergin

WINDMILL
BOOKS
New York

Published in 2012 by Windmill Books, LLC
303 Park Avenue South, Suite #1280, New York, NY 10010-3657

Editor: Rob Walker
U.S. Editor: Sara Antill

Library of Congress Cataloging-in-Publication Data

Bergin, Mark.
 Safari animals / by Mark Bergin. — 1st ed.
     p. cm. — (It's fun to draw)
 Includes index.
 ISBN 978-1-61533-348-6 (library binding)
 1. Animals in art—Juvenile literature. 2. Wildlife art—Juvenile literature. 3. Drawing--Technique—Juvenile literature. I. Title.
 NC780.B44 2012
 743.6—dc22

2010052093

Manufactured in China

CPSIA Compliance Information: Batch #SS1102WM:
For Further Information contact Windmill Books, New York, New York at 1-866-478-0556

Contents

Zebra

1 Start with the head. Add a dot for the eye.

2 Add ears, a mouth, nostrils, and hair.

3 Draw the neck and a bean-shaped body.

You Can Do It!

Use wax crayons for background texture. Paint over them with watercolor paint. Use a black felt-tip pen for the zebra's stripes.

4 Add the mane and the tail.

Splat-a-Fact

No two zebra's stripes are exactly the same.

5 Draw four legs and hooves.

4

Lion

1 Start with the head. Add two dots for the eyes.

2 Add the nose, mouth, and whiskers. Draw in the mane.

Splat-a-Fact
Lions rest for about 20 hours each day.

3 Add the body with a curly tail and four legs with big paws.

Giraffe

1 Start with the head, mouth, hair, and dots for the eyes and nostrils.

2 Draw two long lines for the neck. Add an oval shape for the body.

3 Add a mane, two ears, and tufts on the horns.

You Can Do It!

Use wax crayons for texture. Paint over them with watercolor paint. Use brown ink for the giraffe pattern and a felt-tip pen for the lines.

Splat-a-Fact

Giraffes are the tallest animals on Earth.

4 Draw four legs and a tail.

9

ostrich

1 Start with the head.
Add a beak and
a dot for the eye.

2 Draw two lines
for the neck.

3

Draw an oval shape with
a flat bottom for the body.
Add a line at the front
and the wing.

4 Add two legs with clawed
feet and big tail feathers.

you Can Do It!

Use oil pastels and
use your finger to
smudge them. Use
a felt-tip pen for
the lines.

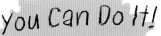

10

11

Eagle

1 Start with the head and the body.

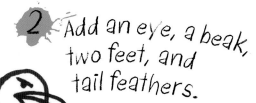

2 Add an eye, a beak, two feet, and tail feathers.

3 Draw two wings.

You Can Do It!

Use wax crayons for the feather shapes and textures. Paint over them with watercolor paint. Use a felt-tip pen for the lines.

Splat-a-Fact

Eagles have excellent eyesight and razor-sharp talons.

4 Add the feathers of the wings.

12

Wildebeest

1 Start with the head and the horns.

2 Add two ears and dots for the eyes and nostrils.

splat-a-Fact
A wildebeest is also called a gnu (noo).

you Can Do It!
Add color with watercolor paint. Use a sponge to dab more color on for added texture. Use a felt-tip pen for the lines.

3 Draw the body shape and neck.

4 Add four legs and a tail.

14

Elephant

1 Start by cutting out the shape of the head.

2 Cut out the tusk and add a dot for an eye.

3 Cut an oval for the body.

4 Cut out the tip of the tail and four legs. Draw the toenails.

You Can Do It!

Cut the shapes from colored paper and glue in place. The elephant head must overlap the body. Use a felt-tip pen for the lines.

Splat-a-Fact

An elephant is the only mammal that cannot jump.

Make sure you get an adult to help you when using scissors.

16

17

Leopard

You Can Do It!
Use colored pencils and a felt-tip pen for the lines. Use both for the leopard's spots.

1 Start with the head.

2 Add two ears, a nose, a mouth, and a dot for an eye.

3 Draw the neck and the body.

4 Add whiskers and a tail.

Splat-a-Fact
Leopards are great climbers. They like to eat and sleep in trees.

5 Draw four legs and paws.

18

Warthog

1 Start with the head and a dot for the eye.

2 Draw the neck, hair, tusks, and ears.

Splat-a-Fact

A warthog kneels on its front legs to eat.

3 Draw the body shape.

You Can Do It!

Use a dark pencil for the outline and add color with watercolor paint.

4 Add four legs, a tail, and two dots for nostrils.

Thomson's Gazelle

1 Start with the head and add a dot for the eye.

2 Draw two horns, ears, a nose, and the cheek marking.

3 Add the neck.

4 Draw an oval-shaped body, a tail, and body markings.

You Can Do It!
Use colored pastel pencils and smudge the colors with your finger. Draw the outline with a felt-tip pen.

5 Add the tail and four black-tipped legs.

Splat-a-Fact
A Thomson's gazelle has excellent eyesight, hearing, and sense of smell.

Crocodile

1 Start with the head.

2 Add a nostril, an eye, teeth, and two small bumps.

3 Draw two lines for the body. Add a tail and a line for its belly.

you Can Do It!
Use colored inks and a felt-tip pen for the lines.

4 Add four legs and spikes on its back. Draw lines across its belly and above the eye.

24

Baboon

1 Start with the head and chest.

2 Add the body and lots of fur.

3 Draw the tail, one ear, and dots for the eyes and nostrils.

You Can Do It!
Use wax crayons for texture. Paint over them with watercolor paint. Use a felt-tip pen for the lines.

4 Add two front legs and two back legs.

26

Hippo

You Can Do It!
Color the hippo with watercolor paint. Use a felt-tip pen for the lines.

1 Start with the head and two dots for the eyes.

2 Add two ears and a mouth.

3 Draw a big oval body.

4 Add a tail and four legs with toenails.

Splat-a-Fact
Hippos spend most of the day in water. They do not swim, though.

28

Cheetah

1 Start with a head.

2 Draw a dot for the eye. Add the mouth.

3 Add a long, oval shape for the body. Draw two lines for the neck and a dot for the nose.

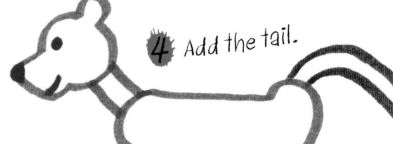

You Can Do It!

Draw the outlines in brown felt-tip pen. Color in with colored pencils.

4 Add the tail.

Splat-a-Fact

A cheetah can run about 75 miles per hour (121 km/h)!

5 Add four legs.

Read More

Haas, Robert. *African Critters*. Des Moines, IA: National Geographic Children's Books, 2008.

Hodge, Susie. *Animals*. Let's Draw. New York: Windmill Books, 2010.

Walden, Katherine. *Warthogs*. Safari Animals. New York: PowerKids Press, 2009.

Glossary

beak (BEEK) The hard mouth of a bird or a turtle.

nostril (NOS-trul) One of the openings to the nose.

smudge (SMUJ) To blend together.

talons (TA-lunz) The strong, sharp-clawed feet of a bird that eats animals.

texture (TEKS-chur) How something feels when you touch it.

tusk (TUSK) A long, large pointed tooth that comes out of the mouth of some animals.

Index

Web Sites

For Web resources related to the subject of this book,
go to: www.windmillbooks.com/weblinks and select this book's title.